Loughrea's Marathon Man

How I ran 100 Marathons all around the world

Jarlath Fitzgerald

Copyright © 2014 Jarlath Fitzgerald

All rights reserved.

ISBN: 1495363813
ISBN-13: 978-1495363818

DEDICATION

For my family: Teresa, Maurice, Noel, Alan and Fiona.

CONTENTS

	Acknowledgments	i
1	How it all started	1
2	Running the world	6
3	How I run	13
4	The marathons	27

ACKNOWLEDGMENTS

Thanks to my aunt, Sr. Philomena Flynn, who suggested I write this book, and thanks to my friend David Quinn for his help and support, and to John Hearne, who helped with the writing and production.

1 HOW IT ALL GOT STARTED

The town

I was born and reared in the town. My mother's from Loughrea and my father came originally from Ballina. He passed away eight years ago, in early October. I have three brothers and one sister. My oldest brother Maurice is a cop in New York. Noel is next to him. He lives in New Jersey. He's married to an American but her parents are from Tuam. Noel works in a bank. Alan, my youngest brother, has been in England for a good few years and then the youngest, my sister Fiona, is living in Craughwell and she's married with one child.

The interest in athletics began in St. Brendan's Boys School when Noel and Alan started running. Noel is the type of person that could do any sport. He was a good rugby player, he was a good footballer, he tried a bit of boxing. Alan played a bit of rugby, and then later, he got into running.

There's a big rivalry between Noel and Alan. The one time all three of us ran together was a half-marathon in Reading. There were a couple of minutes between them in the end, but Alan still won.

I ran my own race.

When I went on to St. Brigid's Vocational School, I did a lot of cross country training, though I never ran cross country. I wasn't into it. At the time, I liked the shorter distances and I didn't think I'd be strong enough for cross country.

There used to be a running league in town one time, between Loughrea, Balinasloe and Craughwell. We go to their place and run against them, and they'd come to our place and run against us. Around that time, Mary Barrett, an Englishwoman married to a man from Loughrea, came to the town. She's a great coach, and I started running with her. That's what really kicked it all off. In my early teenage years I was short and fast, and I won a lot of 100m and 200m races.

When I got to a certain stage, the next place to go was juniors and these were serious guys. They had spikes and all that. I couldn't go any faster, so I ended up coming last in the races. I changed tack then, and started doing a bit of rugby. But in the rugby, the step up from juniors to seniors was very big. I wouldn't have been able for the hardship.

Heart's in the right place

When I was smaller, I had a lot of problems health-wise. I had, and still have, asthma, and that came against me. But the main problem is something called Kartagener's Syndrome. My heart is on the right, not the left like everyone else. Noel is the same way. It's a rare enough thing, but very unusual that two people from the one family should have it. Noel gets away with all the sport, but I wasn't as lucky.

It holds me back a bit because I'm prone to chest infections, and I get a cough like I smoke 40 Silk Cut, though I don't smoke at all. It's the way the lungs are, they're not able to shift the phlegm. The damp weather here doesn't help. Noel finds the weather in the States suits him a lot better.

No one ever told me not to run because of it. When I started, I found I was able for it, so I just kept going. I've two inhalers and tablets to take, and as I get older, I'm seeing more doctors. I've a check-up every six months. They test your breathing. Sometimes they'll do a scan to make sure everything is ok, but so far, so good.

Fog is the only thing that stops me. I can't run in fog, the chest can't take it.

Watching telly

It was October 1988, I was sitting down watching the Dublin City Marathon, and I said I'd like to do that. Up 'til that point, I'd been doing a bit of running, just to keep myself fit. I had a loop of three or four miles that I'd do twice a week, but you need a goal to keep yourself going, so I said I'd aim for Dublin.

The first race I ran was a half marathon out in Carraroe. I remember I did it in about 1:40, which I thought was good enough for a first time out.

I wasn't involved in the club at the time, I didn't know anyone who ran, other than the brothers. I went out with them one time, sure they ran the shite out of me. I've never done speed work, and I never will because I'm not able for it. That's like 200m around the track flat out, then a slow lap to recover, then flat out again. I've never ever done that, I hate it. For me, speed work is go out and run as hard as I can in a race. I get the strength for doing that by doing ten and fifteen mile runs, to build up the stamina.

Starting Out

When I started training for the 1990 Dublin City Marathon, I didn't really know where to start. But there's a magazine called *Irish Runner* that comes out every couple of months. Normally there's a schedule in it for the Dublin marathon. They give you a six month breakdown of what you should be doing to get yourself ready for the race.

They would say, 'Do five miles Monday, do six miles Tuesday, do seven on Wednesday, do six again on Friday, take a rest on Saturday and do ten or twelve miles on Sunday...' They had it all plotted out over the six months. The race is in October, so usually you start building up in April. That's what I did, more or less. And it stood to me.

I flew through the Dublin Marathon in 1990. I ran it in 3:27. That's when the bug hit me. I knew then that I wanted to do more of them. If that had gone another way, if I'd run it in 4 or 4.5 hours, I'd have said feck this, I'm not doing that again. I'd have thrown my hat at it.

I was fine after it, but you'd know going down the stairs the day after a marathon. The thighs and the calves would be tight. The local races are alright, but the ones you have to travel back from, they're a bit tougher. Sitting on a plane for a few hours coming home isn't ideal. I might be alright for a day or two, then it hits me.

I just run my own race, I go as fast as I can but I can't do any more. I'm not prepared at my age to do heavy training. For me it's just getting from A to B. The fastest marathon I ever ran was 3.24, in Malta in 2004. I was averaging 3.36 for a few years. Every runner goes through a purple patch. Mine was in 2008. I ran four marathons in two months – three in 3:46 and one in 3:47 – and I only lost a minute in the last one because it was in Leicester and there was a bit of a hill at the end. Four in two months. I couldn't do that now, I'd need six weeks to recover. When you're young, you don't think anything of it.

Learning your rhythm

After a while, I stopped following the magazine and worked out my own training plan. The mag would say do ten miles but I might only do eight and leave the ten to another day. You listen to your body. You'd know yourself how you feel before you go for a run. Some days I mightn't do as much but I would make up for it again. Every second week, they said to do a long run. I wouldn't always be able for that because I think you need time to recover. I'd usually leave three weeks between long runs, because that's what *I* need.

It's harder to train in the winter because it's constant bad weather. It might rain during the summer, but it won't be as bad, and you don't have to deal with the dark nights.

When I started out, I used to do laps of the town – two 2.5 mile loops, but that was all on concrete. This was before we had our own track. I would also go over to the Fairgreen – five laps there is a mile, and that's on grass, so you're not doing as much damage to your knees. But after a while you'd get pissed off with that too. You'd start losing count. Was that nine laps or ten?

It took a while to learn my own rhythm. When I was starting out, I'd go out doing runs that I wasn't up to. I'd often have to stop running and walk home. It was too soon, I wasn't ready for it. Get to know yourself, that's the key to it. That's what I told my sister Fiona when she was training for the Dublin City Marathon two years ago. She said herself that the routine in the magazines started easy enough but suddenly got very hard. She had a young child at home at the time and wasn't fitting in as much training as she wanted to. I told her to slow down, take as much time as she needed. She ended up running it in 4:17, which was very good, but she found the last two miles tough. I was running along with her and I asked how she was doing and she couldn't answer. That's a bad sign.

There are so many people running now. On a Tuesday evening in Loughrea, there could be thirty women out. A few years ago, you wouldn't have had ten. People are much more conscious about their fitness and their health. It's great to see them out.

2 RUNNING THE WORLD

The list

The idea to run in different countries came a few years after I had started running marathons. There's another magazine called *Distance Running*. In the middle of the magazine, there's a calendar of running events all round the world. They will say where the race is, whether it's a 10K or a half marathon or a full marathon, and there'll be a number beside it which will correspond with a one of the pages at the back with all the websites, phone numbers and so on. When I saw that, that's when the idea took root. Why not run races around the world?

So that's what I did. I built my life around running marathons overseas. I started making a list of all the marathons I wanted to run. Each time I did one, I'd cross it off the list, but the list is as long as my arm now, and I've had to stop getting the magazine because, well, you have to draw the line somewhere. For every one I was crossing out, I was adding two more.

My holidays went on marathons and nothing else. If I needed to go out foreign, I'd usually need four days. I'd head out Friday, rest Saturday, run Sunday and fly home on Monday. Sometimes the flights didn't work out too well. When I went to Kenya last year, I had to leave the Thursday and didn't get back 'til the Tuesday.

I love to travel, I love to see the world, I don't want to end up saying, 'Oh why didn't I go there?' There are so many different places that I want to go to.

The only real reason I choose one place over another is whether or not I've been there. Kenya was easy because the top runners come from there. Singapore was just a place I hadn't been; it's as simple as that. If I haven't been there, it goes on the list. It might take me two or three years to get to it, but I usually get there in the end. I've planned up to 2016, when I'll be fifty. Over the next few years, I'm hoping to get to Cuba, Portland Oregon, Riga, Seattle, Macedonia, Morocco, Estonia and Bucharest. I might never get to some of them, but I'll try.

Marathon running is very heavy on the system, and it's a bad mix with long-haul flying. I went across the Atlantic four times in the one year, and that was tough going. I'm not a nervous flier. If something happens, it happens. I don't like hitting those rocky air pockets though. They always seem to come when you're having tea or water. I hate that. You're trying to balance the cup and you spill it in your lap, and you put your hand over it to stop it spilling and next thing you know, you've nothing left.

I can never sleep on a plane. I try to get as comfortable as I can, and I always ask for a window seat so I can lean back, and so I won't be disturbed by people getting out to go to the toilet. But I never sleep. I remember coming back from Mumbai, I watched three different films. I couldn't sleep a wink. As soon as one was over, I put on another one, then another one, just to pass the time.

After Dublin

After Dublin, I wanted to do London, but the way they fell – Dublin in October, London in April – meant that I had to aim for the 1992 London Marathon, eighteen months later. The race itself went fine, but after that, I made a big mistake. I tried to do Dublin again in October, and that meant that I took no break in training, but kept going all the way through the summer. I died after sixteen miles and ended up having to walk the rest of it. I was too inexperienced to know that you can't pack them in like that. You need to take a break.

Early mistakes

That wasn't the only mistake I made in the beginning. The shoes were wrong at the start. One of the first mistakes I ever made was I went on a 10 mile run in shoes that were far too light. My feet were destroyed with blisters afterwards. Now I use a good pair of runners and I put Vaseline on my feet if I'm doing twenty miles or more. You learn all these things at the start. You have to put Vaseline on your nipples or the friction from the t-shirt will be a problem. I often see people with big blood stains there on their shirt. You learn these things after a while.

I learned my lesson after doing the second marathon in 1992 and realised I'd have to build it up slowly. But I was getting fitter, I was running well, and I knew I could try a bit more. I did three in 2000, and three again in 2001. I got to know my body better. I got to know when I could train a bit less and then be fresher going into the race. Why would you be dong more than you should be doing? You learn what you can get away with.

Pacing Yourself

You're still talking about doing thirty miles a week handy...Three sixes during the week and maybe a twelve on a Sunday. Or you might mix it around a bit. Instead of a six, you'll do an eight, and you wouldn't do a full twelve every Sunday. It all balances up. A couple of days before a race you'd do two short runs to keep yourself fresh. So I was getting away with doing less training. They weren't taking as much out of me as I was getting used to them.

You'd know how well you were going recover straight after a marathon. You'd feel good after it, you'd know that you could run a couple of days later. At this stage, I know myself very well, and I never push harder than I know I can go. If it's a short race, I'll run a 7 minute mile and for a marathon, it'll be 8 or 9 minutes.

That's the secret to it, pace yourself. You'll often see people going off like the hammers of hell, and maybe ten or twelve miles later on you'll pass them by and they're walking. I keep the same pace the whole time, it's just what I feel comfortable running at.

I tend to get very consistent times. You might lose a bit at the start with the crowd being bunched in together but once you get out a couple of miles, they're a bit more spread out. Let the people who want to tear off, tear off. I just stay at my own pace and zig zag the slower ones.

Race organisers try to group runners into times. Put all the three-hour runners together, all the four-hour runners together, but you always find people in the wrong categories. Slow runners up there trying to get out quick, for what reason I do not know. There was one woman in the Streets of Galway 8K last year. I can do five miles in 35 minutes, and she was there beside me, telling me she was going to do it in an hour. She had no business being there, she should have been out in the back

Clocking up the numbers

There was a guy in the club called Eddie Reynolds who had done fifteen or sixteen marathons. That put it in my head to build up a few of them. There's another guy called Martin Joyce in Dublin. He's a runner himself, but he also puts together package deals for races around the world. Martin Joyce International Sports Travel. He sorts out the flights, the hotel, the registration for the races. I came across his ad in *Irish Runner* magazine, and ended up doing a load of races with him. Before I knew it, I had fifty marathons done, and that's when I thought I might aim for the hundred.

I started to look at ultra marathons around that time too, the ones that were thirty-five, forty and even sixty miles. There was a famous one in South Africa, the Comrades, that's fifty-six miles. I read about it in one of the running magazines, and thought, yeah I'd like to do that. But you need to build up to fifty-six miles, so there's another one in South Africa called the Two Oceans, which is thirty-five miles, and that's where I started. But the longest one ever was the 100K in Japan in 2004.

Taking too much on

I do make mistakes from time to time, despite all the experience. Three years ago, I ran too many races too close together, I ran them hard and never gave myself time to recover. I ran myself totally into the ground and in the end I had to take six weeks off.

It was the short races that did me in. I did four on four consecutive weekends. Friends would say, 'Will you go to this race?' I'd say, 'Oh I will'. Stop. So I did four over four weekends, between five milers and half marathons. The short races take more out of you because you're running hard the whole time. The last one was ten miles, and I went from running a 7.5 minute mile to running a 10 minute mile. At four miles I was struggling. A friend passed me from the club, he said, 'Come on!' I went a few hundred meters with him and I said, 'Dave go on, I can't go with you.' I just had no energy. I finished it but it took me 1:25. I should have done it in 1:15. I was waiting for my sister to pass me – that would have been bad – but she didn't. She was only three minutes slower than me. She's a nurse herself, and she could see that I was pushing myself too hard.

My iron level went way way down. They put me on iron tablets for three months. They had to, it was gone so low. And I had to take a break.

I take on too much sometimes. I booked to do one in Donegal last October, then I heard about one in Craughwell two weeks earlier. I said, great, I'll do that, but then I worried that I'd get to 16 miles in Donegal and wonder why the hell did I do the one in Craughwell? And there was only a month between the Craughwell one and the 50K in Portumna. As it is, they all worked out ok.

The only reason I did Portumna is I had to drop out of it the year before. I had a really bad day. You know before you go out that you're not going to get far, but you still just give it a go. I felt awful. I felt absolutely awful after one lap. And there were another five to go, so I stopped. When I drop out of a race like that, that will always go down as unfinished business. It will always be there to go back and do it right.

If you start to get into trouble, determination will only get you so far. You can tell yourself that I didn't come all this way not to finish, but there is a breaking point. If you have to stop, you have to stop. You do damage if you stay going. All you can do is try and walk it out, to finish it. You don't pull up unless you're really bad. Twice it's happened to me. In Moscow, and again in Singapore. Singapore was the worst ever. I ended up in a first aid tent with a drip in my arm.

These days, I do three days a week training. I used to run five days a week. If I ran 10 miles on Sunday, I used to run four on a Monday. That's gone now.

Loops and times

I have no preference what time of the year they're on, though heat is tougher to deal with than cold. Cold, you just keep running, but heat is different. You have to get plenty of water, make sure you have your sunblock and a cap on your head. I ran one in Nashville a few years ago and it was sweltering. People were dropping like flies, cramping up and all that. You have to be careful or you'll get heatstroke.

I prefer the one circuit to the ones where you're doing laps. I don't mind getting lapped, but when you keep seeing people passing you again, it's not good. Two laps is ok, but the one in Lithuania last year, the Vilnius Marathon, that was four. That can get monotonous. Boredom comes into it.

It's nice to have a shorter race to break up the marathons. You need a race where you can push yourself a bit for speed work. It's better than doing it out on the road or going around the track. A few short races sharpen you up for the longer runs. I would never run five miles in Loughrea because I just wouldn't have the incentive, but in a race, you have a crowd to keep you motivated. You pass someone out, you see someone in a black t-shirt, and think, I'm going to pass him out. You haven't the same incentive on a training run at home. I know some people do it – I'm going to get to this pole, I'm going to go flat out to the next pole – I never do that, I prefer to go to a short race, where there's a crowd and they'll pull you along.

I'm less interested in times any more. I do it for me. For me, it's to go out and finish my marathon, I'm not looking for any personal goals. If I run 3:50, I run 3:50, if I run 4:10, I run 4:10. Some people say, 'Oh I'm going to break this time,' but I don't.

Addiction

I used to work in dispatch in a place called APW in Galway. I worked at it for twelve years until they folded in 2009. They used to make cabinets for computers and that kind of thing, but they lost out to cheap labour places like Thailand. One day, they called a meeting and said, 'As and from today, the company is no longer in existence'. Up until that point, they were great, they were very good to me. The money was good, and I was able to work all my holidays, my twenty days around racing. Before I did the hundred, I was always trying to cram another one in here and there. On the bank holidays, I'd try to find one in England. If you're living in England you could be racing every day of the week. It's so popular over there. I went over a few times and ran with Alan. He might do a half, I might do a full. I'd go down to his place, we'd have a meal and a chat after the race.

The problem with marathons is they're addictive.

I'm in this 100 Marathon Club and you meet people who are in it and they say where they're going and I say where I've been. We swap stories, 'Oh I'd love to go there'...'Wouldn't it be great to go here...'

I met one woman in Portumna, she was 66 years old and she was after doing 240 marathons. She was there again in Craughwell last year and I'm sure she'll be in Dublin again. I met a fella from Dublin in Craughwell too and he had 49 done in the year so far. In the year! It's addictive.

For me personally, it's the challenge of doing it and doing it in different countries. For me, it's seeing the world. Different environments and so on. I would never go to these places on a normal holiday, I'm not a person who'd go on a holiday and sit off in the sun. It's not for me.

My whole life is about running. In those few years coming up to the hundred, I did nothing except run. I hardly ever went out, I saved everything I had for it. I lived and breathed it. I still do.

I used to go out and drink one time, but once the marathons started, I stopped. I couldn't run and drink, I'd put on too much weight. I used to be 15 stone, I'm only 8.5 now. I used to be too heavy, now I'm too light. I know I'm not eating enough. Whatever I eat, I walk off. I burn off more than I take in. I need to go to a dietician and get my energy levels up. That's probably one of the things that got me so run down. I was burning off calories I didn't have, going into the reserves of fat. Eventually you'll fall apart if you're not replacing what you're eating. You can actually see my ribs now. If you try and pinch me, there's nothing there.

3 HOW I RUN

Fun running

I know it sounds strange but in a way I'm only a fun runner, I'm not into all these strict diets, I do what suits me, I eat what I want to eat. I couldn't be bothered with supplements. If I don't feel like eating, I don't eat. After a marathon, my routine would be go back to the hotel, have a shower, a sandwich, two bottles of coke and a mars bar. All the sugar is for energy. Then I lie down for a couple of hours and then I go out for something to eat. If I don't lie down an hour after a marathon, I'm shagged.

I'm not old but I have a lot of mileage on the clock. I'm twenty-three years running marathons. I can't do what I was doing a few years ago. Two or three is as many as I can do in a year. But I find it hard to stop at two or three. I'm trying to pack in as many as possible before I'm 50. I'll see how I am then. You have to draw the line somewhere. It's easy to say I won't get caught overdoing it, but it's an addiction.

There's the financial side to it too. I can't afford to be off gallivanting around the world. I'm assistant caretaker at the Temperance Hall in Loughrea. The job is part of a scheme that's only going to last four years. When that's up, I might not get another job again. I was out of work for a few years after APW closed. I was at home, doing nothing, and I could be the same again when this scheme ends.

I'll try to pack whatever I can into the marathons now before the job finishes because I could be back on jobseekers allowance again, and that could be reduced further. Maybe things will pick up again in two years' time, who knows?

Preparation

If it's not overseas, it's easier. You try to get to bed early, you have your race gear ready for the morning and your race number pinned on. I try to eat early in the evening, something like pasta, and take on plenty of water. You have to be up early in the morning and have your breakfast two hours before the race in case you have to travel to it. Two slices of toast and a banana, cups of tea. I always bring my own bread with me when I'm away. Hopefully there'll be a kettle in the room, and I might be able to buy milk in a store. Sometimes, the overseas marathons start so early that the restaurant wouldn't be open to get anything and you have to rely on whatever you brought with you.

If I'm doing a race in Dublin, it'll be fish and chips the night before, but pasta if it's local. I won't eat anything too heavy. Some of the marathons have an expo beforehand and they have pasta and things like that, but I'm very fussy when it comes to pasta. I like my own that I cook at home. I do not like red sauce and all that stuff mixed in with it. Mine is plain. Just pasta and a slice a bread with it. I'm always afraid of trying the different kinds of pasta at the expos. If I wasn't doing the marathon, I might chance them, but when I am, I don't want to. When I go abroad, if I can' t find fish and chips, then I'd have a pizza. It mightn't be the best thing to have for a marathon but at least it's familiar.

In Rio, I had pizza because it was the only thing I could find that was suitable. In Lithuania, I went to McDonalds. Chicken Nuggets. Usain Bolt said he got through a hundred chicken nuggets a day at the Beijing Olympics. I said if Usain Bolt can have chicken nuggets, I can have them. I said, feck it, they can't do me any harm.

You have to be careful not to eat too late in the evening. I think that's what happened at the Portumna marathon. I did a stupid thing the day before. I had lunch as normal at one o'clock, then I decided that rather than have to go out too early next day, I'd go back to Portumna to pick up my race number that evening. I got delayed over there and it must have been half seven or eight before I got the pasta on. It was too feckin' late. Instead of having the pasta at lunchtime, which would have been the sensible thing to do, and then come home at seven or eight and have a slice of toast or a bit of bread, I went and did it the other way round. I'd say that's why I felt sick. I wouldn't eat as late again.

I don't sleep well when I'm away, because you're always thinking. There's no clock in these hotel rooms, you're relying on your own thing. You might wake at some point and see it's one o'clock, and then you're awake, counting the hours. You can get a wake-up call but sometimes they frighten the shite out of you. Where's that sound coming from? But I've never overslept. If that happened to me, it'd be a disaster.

I like to have things ready in the morning. I always buy Lucozade Sport and I have that out. I have the bag ready to go. When you're abroad, finding the start of the race can be a problem, especially if it turns out the hotel is far from the course. You try to get one near the start, but that's not always possible. If I get there early enough the day before, I check out where it is and time myself getting there. If I had time, I'd do something touristy. If there was a bus tour of the town, I might take it. A couple of times, there's been a guide there as part of the package. It all depends on how much time there is and if there's anything worth seeing.

When the running starts

A lot of things go through your mind. I'd never get bored, there's always people around you, a bit of chatting. What I've found lately, when I've the 100 marathons T-shirt on me, people notice it. They say, 'Wow, you've done a hundred marathons!' Or, 'How many is this?' You see someone ahead of you and you might ask them how they're doing. You can tell if people on for the chat. I'll have done a race somewhere that they'd like to do, or they'll have done a race that I'd like to do. They might ask, 'How was Cork,' or 'How was Dublin,' but you'll always move on. They'll drop off or you'll drop off. It depends on where you meet them. The further on, the less chat. We usually try to help each other if we can. If someone has a bottle of water, they might turn around and offer it to you, which is very nice. You can get cranky people too, giving out that you're in their way or you're too close to them, but generally, people are alright, they know how hard it is. We're all into the one thing, to get to the finish line in one piece.

I break my race into four quarters, one to six miles, six to thirteen miles, thirteen to twenty miles, twenty to twenty-six miles. That's in my mind. I've the first section done, I'm starting the next section, I'm half way, then I'm thinking about water. There's water every three miles. There might be six water stations in the whole race. I don't take water at the first station, I take the second one. I'm careful not to take on too much water, then when I get to fifteen miles, I don't want any. I want Lucozade Sport, something isotonic, maybe an energy drink. I need to get that into me, then I get to the twenty mile mark, I'm in the last quarter, I'm nearly home.

Sometimes the marathons are in miles, but I like the Kilometres better because there are more of them and they're short. A mile seems very long, a K is not. They come quicker and you know when you get up to 38K, you've only two miles left to go, and that's easy. You know you're nearly there. That works for me, I'm in the zone then.

You're always thinking about how you're feeling, about water and whether to take it or not. You think about what happened in the last marathon, or where you're going next, or you're looking forward to sitting down for a bit. The mind is always ticking over, you can't really shut it off.

You have to be alert too. There's often a lot going on in marathons, especially if there's a big crowd. People are crossing the road, getting in your way. You have to watch that. It's easy to get tripped if you don't watch out. Then there's the water stations. It's alright if they have plastic cups but the danger is that on other days, they might have bottles of water. If you step on them, your foot could go underneath you, or people might be eating orange segments and throwing them away. You have to watch out for them too.

If it's a big marathon, you go off in corrals. You're corralled according to your time; three hours, four hours and so on. And they'll have pacers. Three hour pacers, four hour pacers that you can follow. You have to be in the chute a half an hour before the race starts, then two minutes before, everyone starts stripping off. It's grand if it's a warm day, but if it's cold, there'll be jackets and coats flying all around the place. People drinking water have to throw their bottle somewhere. Often you'll see them wearing plastic bags with arm holes cut out of them, just to keep warm, and when the bell rings, they get taken off and thrown away. You could very easily fall on them.

You'll often see guys dressed up running marathons. In England last year, there were two guys dressed up as Vikings. At another one, there was a guy dressed as Noddy, carrying the car and all. People are crazy like that. Another time, all the firemen were out, carrying a ladder. You always cheer those guys on. It's hard enough for us to do it but to do it dressed up as well, that takes some doing.

You'll get something at the end of every race. Some medals are very plain and straight-forward, some are a bit unusual. After the Rock 'n' Roll one in San Diego, they gave us one in the shape of a guitar. The worst ever was at the Compton 40 mile ultra marathon. All they gave us was a plastic water bottle. And the little medal we got for the Comrades – which was a 56 mile ultra in South Africa – was pretty poor too, when you consider the length of the race.

The future

I've run all sorts of marathons. There were nearly 40,000 runners at the Boston marathon in 1996. I ran one in Donegal last year and there were only twenty in it.

The knees and the hips and the back play up a good bit at this stage. The physiotherapist gave me exercises to help the hips. When I'm sitting at home, I have an awful habit of slouching. I went back to the physio there recently because I was getting tight hamstrings, but it turns out the hamstring isn't tight at all, it's the back. All that sliding down in the chair is doing it no good.

If it gets any worse, I'll have to call it a day, and if that happens, it happens. I'll find it difficult. But if I can't do full marathons, I'll do the half ones. I'll stay running unless my hips get really, really bad. I'll stay running as long as I can.

The other thing that might stop me is this idea that sometimes gets into my head. I'll be running along fine, and I'll start thinking of stopping. It's just a notion gets into my head. You start to feel the legs getting heavy, you might start to get stiff, your calf might start to tighten up...If that happens, I might not stop straight away, but I will stop at some point, and it's always hard to get going again. A few years ago when I was going well, that would have never entered my head. I'd fly through it. If that crack keeps going, I'll have to give up.

I've 110 done now. I've thought about trying to get to 150 by fifty but I don't think the body could take it. I'm not so bothered by the numbers anymore. I wouldn't be able to do sixteen in the one year anymore, like I did in 2008. Financially I couldn't and physically I couldn't.

As a friend said to me last year, 'You've done the hundred, you've no more to prove'. It's true, but I'd still like to travel.

I know roughly what I'll be doing in 2014, but I'll always throw another race or two into it. I'm hoping to do one in Sunderland in the end of April, then two weeks later there's one in Kildare, then I'm doing Dungarvan at the end of June. The overseas one will probably be Cuba in November, because I've been wanting to go there for a while. That's four, but I know there's a 50K up in Wicklow that's off road. That's in March. I might do that. We'll see.

I'm hoping to go to Seattle in 2015 or 2016, and my 50th birthday is on the same weekend as the Dublin City Marathon in 2016, so I'll do that too. When I get to 50, I'll see how things are. But I'll have to stop on an even number. I'd rather do 120 than 121. But I can't see myself doing 130. I have to be realistic at this stage. If it gets to the stage where the enjoyment goes out of it, there's no point doing it.

Running marathons all over the world is an expensive business. The 100th one, in Barbados cost me at least €1,000 for the flight alone. But when

I finish running I can say that's where all my money went to. Some people can't say what they've done with their money. I've travelled the world, and I think it's money well spent.

The only picture of the whole family together. From left to right, it's Maurice, Alan, Noel, myself, Teresa, Fiona and Sean.

Myself in between Alan on the left and Noel on the right.

Philadelphia was one of the coldest marathons I ran. You had to wrap up warm. That's Noel alongside me.

Myself and Alan just before the start of the Shakespeare half marathon in the UK.

Myself and Fiona running the Dublin City Marathon in 2012. The last few miles can be tough.

The Comrades Ultra Marathon in South Africa was fifty six hilly miles. Very hard on the legs. I could feel it for months afterwards.

Myself and with the great Haile Gebreselassie. He has two gold medals for the 10,000 metres and he won the Berlin marathon four times in a row.

You wouldn't know it from the picture, but this was one of the coldest marathons I ever ran. Myself and Noel ran the full marathon that day, and Maurice ran the half.

India was very warm. Plent of sublock and of course the hat. This was my 91st marathon. The end was in sight.

This is the medal I got for completing the hundred from the UK 100 Marathon Club.

And this one came from the Irish 100 Marathon Club.

You get a medal for every race you finish. Some of them are quite unusual. For Donegal last year, it was in the shape of a cow and its eyes lit up when you pressed a button.

Myself, Colette and Noel at the end of the 100th Marathon in Barbados.

4 THE MARATHONS

1 Dublin	1990	Marathon	
2 London	1992	Marathon	
3 Dublin	1992	Marathon	
4 New York	1993	Marathon	
5 Boston	1996	Marathon	
6 Holland	1997	Marathon	
7 Germany	1997	Marathon	
8 Chicago	1998	Marathon	
9 Belfast	1999	Marathon	
10 Dublin	1999	Marathon	
11 New Zealand	2000	Marathon	
12 California	2000	Marathon	
13 Dublin	2000	Marathon	
14 Czech Republic	2001	Marathon	
15 Venice	2001	Marathon	
16 Beijing	2001	Marathon	
17 Stockholm	2002	Marathon	
18 South Africa	2002	Ultra Marathon 35 Miles	
19 2 Bridges, Scotland	2002	Ultra Marathon 35 Miles	
20 Cardiff	2002	Marathon	
21 Washington	2002	Marathon	
22 Dubai	2003	Marathon	
23 Connemara	2003	Marathon	
24 Lausanne	2003	Marathon	
25 Barcelona	2003	Marathon	
26 Paris	2003	Marathon	
27 Speyside, UK	2003	Ultra Marathon 31 Miles	
28 Fife, Scotland	2003	Ultra Marathon 31 Miles	
29 South Africa	2003	Ultra Marathon 56 Miles	
30 Longford	2003	Marathon	
31 Budapest	2003	Marathon	
32 Canada	2003	Marathon	
33 Connemara	2004	Ultra Marathon 39 Miles	
34 Portugal	2004	Marathon	
35 Trieste	2004	Marathon	
36 Copenhagen	2004	Marathon	
37 Edinburgh	2004	Marathon	

38 Sutton, England	2004	Ultra Marathon 31 Miles
39 Saroma, Japan	2004	Ultra Marathon 62 Miles
40 Dublin	2004	Marathon
41 Athens	2004	Marathon
42 Oldbury, UK	2004	Ultra Marathon 30 Miles
43 Malta	2005	Marathon
44 Poland	2005	Marathon
45 Vienna	2005	Marathon
46 Dartmoor, England	2005	Ultra Marathon 32 Miles
47 Kent, England	2005	Ultra Marathon 32 Miles
48 Reykjavic, Iceland	2005	Marathon
49 Belgium	2005	Marathon
50 Russia	2005	Marathon
51 Compton, UK	2005	Ultra Marathon 40 Miles
52 Dublin	2005	Marathon
53 Beirut	2005	Marathon
54 Luton	2005	Marathon
55 Blackpool	2005	Marathon
56 Robin Hood, UK	2005	Marathon
57 Texas	2006	Marathon
58 Mexico	2006	Marathon
59 Serbia	2006	Marathon
60 Brazil	2006	Marathon
61 Kent	2006	Marathon
62 Finland	2006	Marathon
63 Slovakia	2006	Marathon
64 Thailand	2007	Marathon
65 Los Angeles	2007	Marathon
66 Shakespeare, UK	2007	Marathon
67 Longford	2007	Marathon
68 New Forest, UK	2007	Marathon
69 Cornwall, UK	2007	Marathon
70 Jamaica	2007	Marathon
71 Norway	2007	Marathon
72 Loch Ness	2007	Marathon
73 Turkey	2007	Marathon
74 Miami	2008	Marathon

75 Israel	2008	Marathon
76 Philippines	2008	Marathon
77 Windermere, UK	2008	Marathon
78 Clare	2008	Marathon
79 Oregon	2008	Marathon
80 Cork	2008	Marathon
81 Connemara	2008	Ultra Marathon 39 Miles
82 Stevenage, UK	2008	Marathon
83 Rome	2008	Marathon
84 San Francisco	2008	Marathon
85 Longford	2008	Marathon
86 Wolverhampton	2008	Marathon
87 Leicester	2008	Marathon
88 Slovenia	2008	Marathon
89 Hastings	2008	Marathon
90 Philadelphia	2008	Marathon
91 Mumbai	2009	Marathon
92 Cyprus	2009	Marathon
93 Halstead & Essex	2009	Marathon
94 Nashville	2009	Marathon
95 Newry	2009	Marathon
96 Cork	2009	Marathon
97 Dingle	2009	Marathon
98 Croatia	2009	Marathon
99 Niagara Falls	2009	Marathon
100 Barbados	2009	Marathon

New York Marathon, 1993

I hated this one. The race starts in Staten Island, but you're not allowed to go out there yourself. I stayed with my brother Maurice and he dropped me down to the collection point in Manhattan, and that's where you catch a bus out to the start of the race. After that, they close the roads. I was there hours beforehand, just hanging around, eating bagels and drinking coffee.

At one point, I left my gear to go to the toilet and when I came back, it was gone. It was my own fault. I should have left it into the baggage area but instead, I chanced it. When people are hanging around at the start of a marathon, they always bring extra gear so they won't get cold. That just gets abandoned, so there were stewards going around picking up any unaccompanied stuff. There wasn't a whole lot in the bag, except my inhaler, but I was in bad form anyway waiting around and losing it didn't help.

And then of course, they always let the big shots, the elite runners off first, and the rest of us are let off in groups. There's the three hour corral, the four hour corral and so on.

This was my first big overseas marathon, and the first time I had taken a long haul flight. I'd do it with my eyes closed now, but at the time, it was tough going.

The run itself was only alright. We finished up in Central Park. You get directed out to an area where they've a big electronic panel that shows up your initials. F for Fitzgerald and so on. I waited there and Maurice came and picked me up.

Boston Marathon, 1996

This was in the early days. My fifth marathon. I'd done Dublin twice, then London and New York. I needed a break in 1994 because I'd done so much so fast, so I did a half marathon in Amsterdam, and another short one the following year. But I started aiming for Boston – which was in April 1996 – early the previous year.

This was a special one, because they were celebrating the 100th anniversary of the race, and there was a huge field, nearly 40,000 runners. Maurice and Noel came down from New York to see me, which was great. We went to a special mass beforehand, and afterwards, the priest invited all the Irish runners up on to the altar to say who they were and where they were from. There were so many that afterwards, the priest says, "There must be no one left in Ireland at all."

It was a lovely warm day but there was snow still on the ground from a couple of days previously. I enjoyed that run because it was mostly straight. They bring you out, 26 miles outside the city and you run back in. There's a place called Heartbreak Hill at twenty miles and it's very tough. You don't need it after running for twenty miles. But there's a college right there and all the kids were shouting and roaring at us, and that gives you a great boost.

There's a statue in the same place of a man called John A Kelley, who ran 58 Boston marathons, and won the race in 1935 and 1945. He also ran in the Olympics three times. Heartbreak Hill is called that because of him, because he came second in the race seven times.

Berlin Marathon, Germany, 1997

This course is famous for being flat. Wilson Kipsang from Kenya broke the world record here last year when he ran it in 2:03:23. I remember there were roller skaters on that course when I did it in '97 and they were zipping by everyone, weaving in and out. We went through the Brandenburg Gate, and around the roundabout with the Berlin Victory Column in the middle of it. I ran 4:17, and I was happy with it at the time.

I wasn't so happy later on though. I went over with a group from Ireland and the fella I was sharing a room with didn't stop snoring all night. When I got back after the run, he was sitting on the bed wearing one of those silver yokes they put around you after the race to keep you warm. He was in bits. And that night, he snored and he snored and he snored. I said never again. The next time, I'll pay the extra few pound and get a room on my own.

Chicago Marathon, 1998

I went out to this one on my own. My mother dropped me down to Shannon and Noel flew down and met me at the airport. Noel is way faster than me. He's a 3:15 marathon runner and he has twenty something done at this stage. For most of the American races, he's come down and run with me, which is great.

The day of the marathon itself was warm, but the weather turned bad the following day and the plane couldn't get out. I had to ring home and take another day off work. But work at the time were very understanding about the running. In particular, my boss, John Burke gave me a lot of flexibility.

Belfast City Marathon, 1999

I hated it. I remember coming up to the water station and there were about 20 people standing around and your man was filing water form a barrel. A barrel! Normally, the water would be out on tables and you'd grab it as you go by. He wasn't ready for any of us and ended up slowing the whole thing right down. And we had to go through a few housing estates too, which weren't that nice. I finished in 4:10, which was ok, but it could have been a good bit faster if it wasn't for the water situation.

Millennium Marathon, Hamilton, New Zealand, 2000

This was the first marathon anywhere in the world in the new millennium. 2,000 runners in the city of Hamilton on the North Island of New Zealand.

When I started heading off around the world to do marathons, I usually went with the tour operator, Martin Joyce. He's a runner himself and had been taking groups of runners off to marathons for years. He planned to do the Millennium one, and I put my name down and waited to hear back. But in the end, he didn't get the numbers, and I had to find another way to get there.

It was late at this stage, but I got in with an English group. They sorted out the hotel and the registration for the race, but the flights were totally booked out. I remember I sat down the Maurice Sweeney, the travel agent here in town, and we spent ages trying to come up with a route down to New Zealand. We got there in the end, but I had to take four or five flights and of course it cost me an arm and a leg.

We flew out on Christmas Day and had tinsel and turkey and all that on the plane. The good thing was I had plenty of time to recover before the run, which started at 6am so that we could get the first sunrise of the Millennium. Unfortunately, all we got was rain and mist.

The English crowd I was with stayed on English time while they were there and when it came midnight at home, which was hours later, they all started singing Auld Lang Syne.

They did have a few tourist things organised for us. We went to see a

Maori show, and they took us out to a dairy farm. I had a day left to myself afterwards and when I was out walking around Hamilton, this couple stopped me to ask directions. I said, 'Sorry, I'm not from this neck of the woods.' It turned out they were from Belfast and they were into horses. They took me out horseracing that afternoon. The same day, I found a place for a cup of coffee and a bun, and the girl who served me asked where I was from

"Ireland," I said.

"I know that," she says, "what part?"

"Loughrea."

"I'm from Oranmore!"

You never know who you'll run into.

Beijing Marathon, China, 2001

This trip was great crack. Martin Joyce was putting a group together to go to Beijing, which is why I went for it. There were 75 of us, all Irish. They had organised a half marathon and a 10K as well, so there was something for everyone. We walked the Great Wall and went to see a few temples. There's a picture of the lot of us in Tiananmen Square before the start of the race.

I had a great run. 3:27. It was the fastest time I had ever run up until then. I could feel myself getting fitter.

In the restaurants, all of the food was laid out on these big revolving plates. You just took what you wanted. I didn't trust it though. All I ate was rice and chips and the odd Mars Bar, for sugar, when I could get it. I was afraid if I changed my diet, I'd get an upset stomach. I couldn't handle the chopsticks either. I still have a souvenir pair at home in a bag.

We had trouble on the way home. The flight had to divert to Shannon, and it was late in the evening, so there were no busses. I had to get a taxi up home. They lost my bag too. It didn't show up for nearly a week afterwards.

Venice Marathon, Italy, 2001

An expensive spot. I would have gone out in the Gondolas but they were charging rip off prices. But the run itself was nice. I went with an English group. We were bussed out the 26 miles and ran back in. The end of the race was lovely. We went in through the city, which is beautiful, and ran over a few of the canal bridges.

Two Oceans Ultra Marathon – South Africa, 2002

You start off doing your 10 miles, then your half-marathon, then your full marathon. You're always seeing how far you can go, how much your body can take. When you get used to doing marathons, the distance becomes a bit run-of-the-mill. You're always wondering if you could push things a bit farther.

I'd heard about the Comrades Ultra Marathon and I really wanted to do it, but it was 56 miles, so I knew I'd have to build up to it. The Two Oceans ultra marathon in Cape Town is 35 miles. This is one of those ones where as well as seeing the country, I wanted to see if I could do the distance.

Those extra nine miles were tough, and the run was very very hilly, but I had trained well for it. I was doing 30 mile runs at home. There's a 15 mile loop around Loughrea that I'd do twice in the one go, and at the same time, I was doing the odd marathon abroad. I think I did walk a couple of the hills, but I recovered quite quickly from it.

They call the Two Oceans the world's most beautiful marathon, and there is lovely scenery along the route. They run it down along the Cape Peninsula, where the Atlantic meets the Indian Ocean. I knew once I'd finished it that I'd be able for the big one, the Comrades, the following year.

Comrades Ultra Marathon – South Africa, 2003

I didn't do much special training coming up to it, I just ran more miles. I did try and take on more calories in the weeks before it, but I doubt I ate enough. If I'm not hungry, I just can't eat. During a race, I might have a pocket full of jellybabies, or bits of chocolate, an orange or a Mars Bar cut up. But on the Comrades you'd never go hungry. Loads of people had barbeques out along the route and they were offering food to the runners the whole time.

Fifty-six miles. This one was tough. It's very hilly. They run it uphill one year and down the next, but you still gets lots of variation in that. In 2003, they were running it downhill and that was hard on the legs. In fact, I could feel it for months afterwards. We started at four in the morning to avoid the heat and I finished in 10 hours 15 minutes. The cut-off time is 11 hours. There are checkpoints along the route, and if you haven't made it to those points by a certain time, they won't let you go any further. They stop you and put you on a bus.

I remember after I finished, I was waiting at the finishing line to be bussed back, and in the minutes coming up to the cut-off point, there were loads of people lining the route. They were all holding banners and shouting and banging the sides, encouraging the runners to get in ahead of the time. Some of them were in bits, staggering and weaving all over the road. They let in the ones who were a couple of minutes over, but they stopped the ones who were just too slow.

Cardiff Marathon, Wales, 2002

Worst accommodation ever. It was a B&B right opposite Cardiff Arms Park. They put us sleeping in one house, but you had to have your breakfast next door. I've stayed in a few kips over the years, but this one was the worst. The bedroom was tiny and a bit of a mess. I think they were taking advantage because they knew the marathon was on. The run itself went grand, but the marathon itself hasn't really got off the ground. It's only a half-marathon these days.

Marine Corps Marathon, Washington DC, 2002

I liked Washington. It wasn't long after September 11 and there were big fences up all around the Pentagon. My brother Noel and his wife Ann drove down from New York and we got a tour around the day before.

This was the closest I ever came to beating him. Noel was always the athlete in the family. He was good at anything he tried, hurling, football, boxing, rugby...That day I was in good form and running well, running at my own pace. Noel started off great, but he slowed and slowed as we got closer to the end. At one point, the course doubles back on itself, and you could see the runners ahead of you coming against you on the other side of the road. There was Noel, and he was starting to struggle. Seeing me so close behind him probably gave him a bit of a boost and he managed to get in a few minutes ahead of me. Almost had him.

Barcelona Marathon, Spain, 2003

The expo is the big event they put on the day before, where you've all the different shoe companies with stands and you register for the race and so on. The Barcelona Marathon was only a couple of years old and their expo was one of the smallest, most basic ones I've ever been at. I ran very well that day though. 3:27. Some days you just hit form.

Lausanne Marathon, Switzerland, 2003

I flew into the wrong city and never copped it until it was too late. I was heading for the Lausanne Marathon, but went to Lucerne instead, which is about a hundred and fifty miles north.

I got there the day before the marathon, and found a fast train that could get me down on time. But after the race, everyone was heading back on the same train, and it filled up before I could get on. I was wrecked after the race, all I wanted to do was lie down, but I had to wait a couple of hours in the station for another train. Plus I had to be up early the next morning to get another train to the airport.

Eventually, I got back to the hotel in Lucerne, set the alarm and went to bed. When I got up the next day and went down to check out, the receptionist told me that the clocks went back the night before. Wasn't I after getting up an hour before I had to. So I had to go back up to the room for an hour to wait for the train. Sometimes, I'm just not tuned in and things like this happen.

The Fife Marathon, Scotland, 2003

I ran Connemara, Paris and Fife on three consecutive weekends. I was fit and confident, I felt I was strong enough to put them that close together. The one in Fife was 50K, and that was made up of fourteen loops of the town. Each time, you came back to a racetrack and there was a guy there in a tent keeping track, telling you how many laps you'd done, so you wouldn't end up doing fifteen instead of fourteen. When I got my times afterwards, it turned out that I'd run thirteen of them in the exact same time, and one slightly faster. I couldn't believe it. I was after getting really consistent without realising it.

Speyside Way Ultra Marathon, Scotland, 2003

Another ultra, way up in the north of Scotland. I flew into Aberdeen and then took a bus up to a place called Lossiemouth which is right on the sea. I ran well, but a few times I had to slow right down because it was off-road and wasn't all that well marked.

Toronto Marathon, Canada, 2003

They put on a half marathon the same time, and this was the first time Maurice tried that distance. He came up from New York with Noel, and myself and Noel ran the full marathon. It was probably the coldest one I ever ran. I'll never forget that.

That night, we had to go down to reception to ask to be moved off the floor because there had been some sort of hockey tournament on the same weekend and the kids were all celebrating in the rooms beside us. We couldn't get a wink of sleep.

Connemara International Marathon, 2003, 2004, 2008

Connemara is tough. It's just so hilly. And then there's the weather. The first year I did it, it was lovely and sunny, but the last time, in 2008, I hadn't gone maybe half a mile before the hailstones started. It was bitterly cold, and the route is really exposed. There was a wind coming in off the Atlantic that would cut you. I remember pulling down my sleeves against the weather. It's hard enough to do the distance without the bad weather down on top of you too.

Getting wet early on is bad. It you get one shower, it dries into you, if you get another on top of that, you could get pneumonia out of it. You just put up with it, there's nothing else you can do.

The last two miles are like an 'S'. You get to the top of a hill and you can see Peacockes of Maam Cross in the distance. That's when you know you're not far away.

The ultra is a real challenge. It's forty miles, which is the most I've ever run without stopping. It's often in my head now, could I run a couple of miles more? There's a fifty mile somewhere, but I doubt I'd be able to keep going for another ten miles. I might get away with four or five, but I don't think I'd chance ten.

Running uphill is alright. You put the head down, pump your arms a bit more and you'll get up there eventually. Downhill is tougher. You put more pressure on the backs of your legs going downhill. I tend to hold myself back for the drops, and my calves get tight.

Fair play to them, at the end, they have a big tent with sandwiches and tea and soup. The last year, I was shaking for half an hour afterwards, it was that cold. Two of the girls on duty saw me and came over, and once I had the soup in me and was back in dry clothes, I was alright.

In 2008, I was getting close to the hundred, so I was trying to rack up every one that I could. Connemara was local, so it looked like an easy one, but of course getting out there from Loughrea was nearly as much hassle as going abroad. The busses were leaving from the Cathedral in Galway at 8am, so I had to get a bus in from Loughrea an hour earlier to be there on time. And even when you got into the cathedral, you were waiting around for ages for the bus to fill so you could head off. It was the same then in the evening, waiting around so you could get back to Galway. It was very late by the time I got home.

Cornish Marathon, England, 2007

Worst weather ever. Down in the south of England. It rained and rained and rained all day. It was miserable and cold and a lot of it was high up and exposed too. You just have to have the right clothes on you and you just have to keep going. Puddles are the worst. That happened last year in a 10K in Athenry. It rained so much there were floods, some of them going across the whole road. You never know how deep they are, or what potholes could be hidden under the water, so the only thing to do is go right through the middle. So your feet are soaking and its squish squash the rest of the way.

Dubai Marathon, 2003

This was a great trip, though I had a lot of hassle at the start. I flew out on my own, but I had booked to join up with an English group. I arrived late in the evening, and the hotel was looking for money, even though I'd already paid through the group. I ran into an English guy with the same problem and he sorted us both out, but then the hotel wanted to hold on to my passport, and I needed it to register for the race the next day. At that hour of the evening, after a very long flight, it was the last thing I needed.

The run itself went grand. They started early in the morning to avoid the sun. I couldn't get a flight back straight away, so I had a few days out there. The first morning, we went off out on jeeps over the sand. That was great crack. We had a meal out in the desert. They have a funny way of greeting each other out there, they rub their two noses together. It's great when you get to go to different places before and after the marathon, and do different things. Any chance I get to do something different, I take it.

Saroma 100K Ultra Marathon, Japan, 2004

This was my longest ever run. 62.5 miles, 100 Kilometres. I didn't do much to change my training coming up to it. The races I was running were enough of a build-up. I ran the Two Oceans, which was thirty-five miles in 2002, and the Comrades, which was fifty-six miles in 2003. Both were in South Africa. To be honest, I couldn't do much more training because my knees were bad for a couple of years after the Comrades, probably because of all the downhill running. I had to let my body recover.

I don't think I could say that I enjoyed that run. I just wanted to get through it, to get to the finish line. I wasn't thinking of anything else. It started early in the morning, and you had 13 hours to complete it. There were checkpoints along the way, and if you didn't make them within a certain time, they'd stop you and put you on the bus. I ran a bit, I walked a bit and got through it in 12.5 hours.

It was also the longest flight I had ever done. Twelve hours. I was very tired from all the travelling before I got there, so I wasn't in the best form doing the race itself. Despite the distances – flying and running – this was another three day job. Fly in, run, fly home. I had so little time that I didn't get to walk around the city at all. I just went back to the hotel and crashed. I think there was a vending machine outside in the hall. I went out and got a couple of Mars Bars out of it.

Often, when I go away, that's what I live on. Mars Bars and coke, and a bit of bread in the morning. It works for me.

Athens Marathon, Greece, 2004

I ran the Dublin City Marathon on the Monday, then flew out a few days later to do Athens. This was the same year as the Olympics, and we were following the same route – there was a blue marker on the road that marked the course, and it ended up in the Olympic Stadium.

I found an ad on one of the English running magazines that I buy where someone was offering accommodation in their own home. They met me at the airport, brought me out to the race, collected me at the end and then dropped me to the airport the following day. Very handy.

Sutton Ultra Marathon, England, 2004

This was made up of laps of a park. 31 miles or 50K. It started off early in the morning, and that was fine, but after a couple of hours it opened to the public and next thing the park started to get very busy with people, and we had to dodge and weave around them. That was a pain. You don't want all your energy going on twisting and turning, especially when it's an ultra. I remember I had to walk some of it because of that.

This was one of the few times I flew home the same day. Normally, I'd get back to the hotel, shower and lie down for a bit, but this time, my mother dropped me out to the airport in Galway and I flew out, left my bag in the changing room and went straight back to the airport from the race.

Edinburgh Marathon, Scotland, 2004

This was great, because some of us from the club had been over to see the European Cross Country Championships the previous December. That was a great weekend. They put on a 5K run in the morning, and after that, we went back to the hotel, had our breakfast, checked out, left our luggage in the baggage area and went off to the cross country. It was great to see Paula Radcliffe in action. She won that day, though the Irish women came second in the team event, and Sonia O'Sullivan ran very well.

I knew I was coming back for the marathon in May, so I booked the hotel before we left. It was only a ten minute walk from where the marathon started, and it was great to know where I was going for a change.

I flew back the night of the marathon too. The flights just suited. I checked in, had my dinner in the airport, flew back to Dublin and got the bus down to Loughrea. I was wrecked after it.

Beirut Marathon, Lebanon, 2005

I saw it on a list in one of the English running magazines I read, or I saw an article about it and I just said I'd like to do it. I'll never forget it. There were soldiers everywhere. Everywhere. At one stage, I had to stop to get sick and one of them came over to me to see if I was alright.

That happened a few times that year. It was the year my father died and I ran fourteen marathons. So I was in and out of the hospital visiting him, and I was training hard, so I suppose the whole thing came to a head. Something had to give. I got sick running the Dublin City Marathon too, though I put that down to the weather. It rained and rained and rained. I was soaked before I even started, and at the twenty mile mark, I had to stop and throw up.

Anyway, the run in Beirut went fine. It was November, it was sunny, but not too hot. The only thing was, afterwards, you had no comfort walking around with people hassling you to buy stuff. 'Do you want to go here...Do you want to buy this...' There were taxies stalking you looking for business and all I wanted to do was walk around and get a feel for the place.

I remember going to one place and there was a fella selling me something, so I walked across the road, straight into another fella. I hate that. They say that they want to welcome visitors to these places but then they go and hassle you all the time. People won't come back there if they can't walk around without being hassled.

Omsk Marathon, Russia, 2005

This was unfinished business. The previous year, I flew out to Moscow in Russia to do the marathon, but I wasn't well. I had a bad enough chest infection, and the week coming up to it, I got a cut in work, and that got infected too. I had this finger dressing on it. By the time I got to the airport, the chest infection was after turning into the flu, but I had the whole thing paid for so I couldn't just not go. I said I'd chance it, even if I had to walk it. But I felt so bad halfway, I realised that there was no point going on. If I had stayed, I think I might have collapsed. I just pulled up, got my gear, went back to the hotel and curled up in the bed for a while.

The thing is, you know when you're going through a bad patch in a race whether you'll get through it or not. Experience will tell you. I knew I couldn't go on, so I just stopped.

If I don't finish a race, I always have to go back and give it another go, so in 2005 I booked with an English crowd to go out to the Siberian International Marathon in Omsk. It wasn't Moscow, but it was still Russia.

If you get into a bad patch when you're running, it helps sometimes to focus on someone in front of you, and follow them. In Omsk, there was a girl running behind me, and I think that's what she was doing with me. I've no problem with anyone following me, only she kept getting too close, and she clipped me three times. She kept saying something in her own language – I suppose it was 'sorry' – but that was no good to me, I nearly fell every time. So in the end I had to stop and let her go on. I took a break, had a drink a water, and off I went again, but damn it if I didn't pass her again, and she got in behind me again and clipped me again. I figured it must have been her first marathon and she just needed the support. So I just tried to ignore her and kept going as best I could.

There were four of five of us on the tour, and a guide who met us at the airport brought us around and made sure everything went well. It didn't go so well in the airport on the way back though. We were just going through security with the bags when two customs guys called me over. They went through all my stuff and then started telling me that my paperwork wasn't right. The guide, who was a Russian girl, came over and she figured out what was going on. They wanted a bribe. A hundred Euro. I told them I didn't have it. I needed money to get the bus home from Dublin airport, but they wouldn't take no for an answer, so in the end I gave them fifty Euro. I had to put it down under this book they had on the desk. I'd never go back there again.

But the good news was that this was No. 50. I was half-way to the hundred.

Reykjavik Marathon, Iceland 2005

I ran a good race that day. 3.43. It was showery, but not as cold as you'd expect for Iceland. Because of the flights, I had a couple of extra days out there, so I went whale watching. I'll never forget that. It was very very rough, and everyone the boat was sick. We were out for ages but saw no whale.

Malta Marathon, 2005

This was my personal best. 3.24. I was in good form, running well and the course was reasonably flat. I went with an English group and we had a guide that met us, arrange the taxies and brought us out to registration and to the race. This was February, so it was warm without being hot. The course itself was a loop. You started out in the capital, Valetta, and ran out and around and back in. I remember there was donkey shit on the road at one point, and we had to dodge that. They had a half-marathon as well, which started after us, and as we got to the end, the fast guys from the half marathon started to come flying past us. It ended up in a bit of a traffic jam, with the half-marathoners getting more and more impatient and roaring at us to keep to one side.

Vienna City Marathon, Austria, 2005

I lived on sandwiches and coke that weekend, because when I got the taxi in from the airport, it cost €40. I hadn't budgeted for that much, and if I was going to keep another €40 to get back out to the airport again, that meant no proper meal.

It was alright, I got by.

It turned out to be a very hot day and there was a big crowd. The course twisted and turned a lot, and there were cobblestones too, which aren't very kind to the knees. I still ran well, in a time of 3.36, which is pretty fast for me. The funny thing is I stopped two miles from the end and started walking. And it was hard to get going again. I have the certificates at home and they show the times I got at all the 5K markers; 5, 10, 15 and so on. I was running great until I stopped, so I was a bit annoyed with myself. I could have run 3.30 or better if I hadn't pulled up.

That just happens sometimes. I switch off for no apparent reason. I just stop. I don't know why. If things are going well, I just fly though it, but if I get it into my head about stopping, I mightn't stop there and then, but I will eventually, if only for a couple of minutes. It doesn't happen every time. If it did, I'd have to seriously think about stopping altogether, because it totally defeats the purpose of doing a marathon. I'm a guy who likes to stay running the whole time.

London Marathon, 1992

The thing about London is it's huge, the largest in the world. You'll have more than 35,000 finishing the race. That gives it a great atmosphere, but the crowds are so big and the roads are so narrow, you're constantly bumping into people. Or they're bumping into you.

You're trying to keep a certain rhythm, and when someone puts you off, it's not nice. Early in the race, you're fresh, you can take it, but when it happens at the end of a race, when you're getting tired, it's very frustrating. When people decide to stop, they just stop dead, and before you know it, you're into the back of someone. If it was less crowded, you might be able to go round them, but it's very easy to hit someone, or to fall yourself.

You can get major problems at water stations. Water stations in a marathon can be at one or both sides of the road. If it's both, you're fine, but if it's one side only, it's desperate, because everyone is heading in one direction, they're all criss-crossing, trying to get to the one place. You'll get people just standing there chatting, drinking the water at the table. I can never understand why they won't take the water and move away from the table and drink it further down, because when you're standing there, you're blocking people coming from behind you.

You're trying to keep going, trying to keep your rhythm up, but if there are people standing there, blocking the way, you might get to the end of the table with no water. And the same thing might happen at the next station, and then you're in trouble, because you haven't taken the water on when you should have.

I always burst my way through if I have to. If I want water, I get it, I don't care who's there, I won't stop. The last day I was out, I saw a guy giving out water, and I shouted at him, 'I want water!' and fair play to him, he had it ready when I ran past.

Compton 40 Ultra Marathon, England, 2005

I did three ultra marathons in 2005. This one took 7.5 hours because I got lost. Not once, but twice. A lot of it was off-road. We were out in the countryside, climbing over stiles and things. When you're running on the road the whole time, it's nice to do something a bit different like that. But my concentration went, there were signs and I missed them. I'd be no good for reading maps, and if there was an arrow showing the way to go, I might easily miss it.

There were people coming behind me and they saw me go off course, and called me back. The other time, I knew I'd gone wrong, so I just stopped and waited for someone to come along. When I got to the next water station, someone said, 'Are you the one who got lost?' You had to get your card ticked at different points along the way, to show that you got there. I have that card at home, I framed it. But I was disgusted that there was no decent prize for finishing. Forty miles and all I got was a water bottle. Not a medal, not a t shirt, but an effin plastic bottle.

Windermere Marathon, England, 2008

The day I ran this one, which is in the Lake District in England, there was a group of people who were finishing up running ten marathons in ten days, all over the same course. And it wasn't an easy course. There was a lot of uphill, and steep uphill at that. I was looking at them at the start, and every single one of them had bandages on their knees or their ankles. That's too much I think, I'd never take on something like that.

Oldbury Marathon, England, 2004

It was very frosty that day and the race had to be delayed for half an hour because the road hadn't thawed out. The route was loops round a power station. They had a guy at one corner and he'd tell you how many you had done and how many you had left to go. This one was really handy too, because the race organiser picked me up from the bus station and brought me to the B&B, then picked me up again the next day and brought me back to the station.

Blackpool Marathon, England, 2005

I'll never forget this one. It was the first time I decided to come home the same day. I was doing a lot of marathons that year and I wanted to keep the costs down, so I said I'd only stay over the night before and come back the night of the race. It was a lovely fine day, but that night, there was a huge thunderstorm and they had to cancel the flight. I had to stay in the airport all night. After running a marathon. I was in bits. I could have got an Aer Arann flight into Carnmore but I hadn't enough cash to get it, and anyway I would have had to get a taxi into Oranmore and then a bus out, but by the time I got there, the last bus would have been gone. I would have been stranded in Oranmore, so I said I might as well stay where I was.

I stretched myself across the seats, what else could I do? I didn't sleep because there's always activity going on in the airport late at night, people coming in early for flights and so on. I said I'd never come home the same day again, though I did after.

Brighton Marathon 2013

I don't drive, so getting morning flights out of Dublin can be a bit of a challenge because the first bus in the morning often goes too late. I went to a marathon in Brighton last April. My flight was at 11am. Normally, you have to be there two hours before the flight so the only way to manage that is to go up the night before and stay in a B&B – which is more money – or get the 1am bus and arrive up into the airport at half four in the morning, and wait. These races are always on a Sunday, and I could have gone up a bit later on the Saturday, but you always need time the day before to register and pick up your number, so I took the last bus and just waited in the airport. I sat in the same spot for about five hours.

That was the Friday night, and the race was Sunday. I'd always stay up and watch *Match of the Day* on Saturday night, but I was so flippin tired that night, I couldn't stay awake. I was in bed by 10. But I ran a very good race the next day.

I've had to do that with the busses a few times – going to Lithuania in 2012 and to Kenya last year. Why pay €70 or €80 for a B&B? It isn't worth it.

Helsinki City Marathon, Finland, 2006

I had a terrible run that day. I felt drained. This was August, so maybe it was all the marathons catching up on me. I ended up walking a lot of it, and it took me six hours. That'll show you.

Kosice Peace Marathon, Slovakia, 2006

The Kosice Peace Marathon is one of the oldest in Europe. It's two laps of the town, and it's great. I really enjoyed this one, and I ran very well too. 3:43. It helped that the hotel was right at the starting point of the race. It often happens that the hotel is miles from where the race starts and you have to go off looking for it and spend money on taxies and so on. Not here.

Rio De Janeiro City Marathon, Brazil, 2006

This was a bit of an adventure. For a start, I missed the flight. I was flying through Paris, and the flight out of Dublin was delayed, which put me under pressure straight away, and Charles De Gaulle is a nightmare if you're taking a connecting flight. You get off the plane, you get on a bus, then you've to get through customs, get on another bus...

So I had to stay the night in Paris and fly out to Rio de Janeiro the next day. I got there eventually and went straight to bed, but weren't they doing a job on the hotel and I got no sleep. They were belting and banging, so I got up and went out to get registered. It all meant I had a shorter time to recover from the flight ahead of the race.

On race day, they bussed us all out to the start, and I remember while we were waiting, there were two groups of fellas over to one side, squaring up to each other, getting ready to fight.

I didn't like the race much, because it was just motorway back into the city, and it was flat and monotonous. Towards the end, we were running along by the beach, and there were people crossing in front of us. One guy was pushing a motorbike along the route. You could do without that after running twenty-three miles

The day after that I went sight-seeing and they brought us up to see that famous statue of our lord. Christ the Redeemer. It was very very steep going up and we had a good walk around it. Anytime I see it on the TV, I say 'I was there.'

LALA International Marathon, Torreon, Mexico, 2006

I had a problem at registration. It turned out that that all of the information I had was about another Mexican marathon. Luckily though, they took my entry.

That day was warm. I remember suffering coming near the end of it, and it was a dusty sort of place too. It was a little town, but I had to walk a bit from the hotel to get to where the race started. They took my name from my passport, and because my second name is Thomas, I ran as Thomas Fitzgerald. In the end, I ran it in 4 hours, which I was happy enough with, given the conditions and the long-haul flight.

Midnight Sun Run, Tromso, Norway, 2007

This is way up at the top of Norway. Tromso is a couple of hundred miles inside the Arctic Circle, though it wasn't cold on the day. It starts at midnight on June 21st, and because it's so far north, the sun doesn't set. It stays bright all night. It's very strange to be going to bed when it's still bright outside.

I'm always keeping an eye out in the running magazines for something different. This one was different. The only problem was you were waiting around all day for it to start. I didn't run a great race. When you're running so late in the day, it's hard to know what to eat. I had pizza and it didn't really agree with me.

Istanbul Marathon, Turkey, 2007

This is the only marathon that takes in two continents. You start in Asia, then run over the Bosphorus Bridge into Europe. I had a good run and finished in 3:43. One of the things that stand out in my memory is the morning gongs, the Muslim call to prayer at 5am.

I didn't have a load of time here so I didn't do anything touristy. But in the taxi on the way in from the airport, the guy was going too fast and didn't he burst a tyre on the curb. I think he was trying to impress me by passing someone out, but I ended up on the side of the road while he changed the wheel.

Los Angeles Marathon, 2007

I didn't enjoy this run. For one thing it was hot. And they bussed us out to the start far too early, so there was way too much hanging around. And the run itself was long and boring. There was nothing to look at.

I had hassle with the hotel too. I checked in grand for the first night, but then on the morning of the race, they told me they were after overbooking and I had to move to another hotel across the road.

Afterwards, I did a bit of touring around. I saw some stars' houses, though we didn't see any stars, only photographers waiting for them to come out. I can't even remember who they were. And I saw the Chinese Theatre, where they have celebrities' handprints in the footpath outside.

America can be expensive. You lose so much money with the tips and that, especially if you're getting taxies here and there. And of course, changing the currency, especially if you go at the wrong time and the Euro is weak.

San Diego Rock 'n' Roll Marathon, 2007

This one was great. They had a different band playing at every mile. It was very hot though, over 30 degrees, one of the hottest I've ever run. You have to wear a cap, and sunblock – I burn very easily. And you have to be very careful about taking enough water on board. It was so hot that I had to stop and walk several times. It was still a really enjoyable race.

The Reggae Marathon, Negril, Jamaica, 2007

Cool, as they say themselves. The Reggae Marathon starts before dawn to avoid the heat, and they have torches out to light the way. It's in a resort called Negril, about two hours from Kingston, which is where I flew in. I took a taxi down, and got a bit of a shock at the fare. It took every cent I had. Luckily, I had my ATM card with me and I was able to take out Jamaican Dollars to keep myself going. I got there very late in the evening, a tiny little place down on the coast, and they told me they would have shut up hours earlier only they were expecting me.

It was a bit rough and ready but it was across the road from the beach.

The race itself was all along the coast, and after I crossed the finish line, I went down and soaked myself in the sea. Beautiful, clear, clean water and not a cloud in the sky.

Khon Kaen Marathon, Thailand, 2007

I had to take four flights to get there. Dublin London, London Istanbul, Istanbul Bangkok, Bangkok Khon Kaen. It was almost as tough as the race. I didn't have long there either. I arrived the Friday, I had Saturday to recover, ran Sunday and then four flights home again on the Monday.

They run it in early January, to avoid the summer heat, but just to be sure, it starts at 4am. I remember we ran though a Chinese area, and there were loads of Buddhist monks out in their robes. I was back in the hotel lying down by 10am. The girl came in to clean the room and I had to tell her, 'No, leave it 'til later, I need to have a rest.'

The hotel itself was grand, but there was nothing but waste ground on either side of it, and there was nothing at all to see in the place itself. I'd never eat the local food in places like this. I'd be afraid it wouldn't agree with me and I wouldn't be able to run. I brought my own bread, wrapped in tin-foil. Bread and tea kept me going. On the way back, I thought to myself, that's another part of the world done.

Rome Marathon, Italy, 2008

I ran sixteen marathons in 2008, the most I'd ever run. I was aiming to get to the hundred the following year, and sixteen would leave me with just ten to do. I knew that if I didn't quite make the sixteen, there'd be enough time left to squeeze another into the following year.

This was the first marathon I'd ever done that they wanted a medical cert to say you were fit to run, and didn't I forget to bring it with me. When I went to register, I got hassle about it. For a while, I thought they weren't going to let me run it. In the end, I had to write out something saying I was fit to do it, so I just about got away with it.

The place I was staying in was like Fort Knox. It wasn't like an ordinary hotel. You had to press a button and go through double doors and up four flights of stairs and through more doors. And there was no restaurant or dining room or anything there. They gave you a voucher and you had to come out through all the doors and down all the stairs and press all the buttons, then go across the street to get a croissant and a cappuccino

The race itself went fine, though I had a job to find the start. In the end, I just followed the crowd.

Clare Burren Marathon Challenge, 2008

It was across the Burren and it was a feckin curse. You started off on the road, but you didn't stay on it. You took off up over the rocks. I fell twice on one shoulder and once on the other knee. I had bruises and I was banged up and I said never again.

Cork City Marathon 2008

This was a very warm day. The course went out around Cork City, and through the Jack Lynch Tunnel. But the heat got to me, and it was the first time I ever got cramp in a race, at 22 miles. I had to stop and the first aid guy came and rubbed my leg, and I got home eventually. It wasn't my best time ever. I blamed the heat. It was so warm, I was losing salt, I could taste it on my arms, and that's a bad sign.

It's always a risk when you run in hot weather that you'll lose too much salt. One tip I was given for running in hot countries was to get a bottle of water and dissolve some salt into it. Start drinking it – just little sips – a few days before the race. I did that before the race in Barbados. The idea is that when you start to sweat, you won't sweat it all out.

Philadelphia Marathon, 2008

I ran four US marathons that year. Philadelphia was one of the coldest ever. There was still frost on the road from the night before and I nearly fell twice. People were drinking water and throwing away what they didn't want, and then that water was freezing over. Parts of the track were like an ice-rink.

Often in marathons, you'll see people throwing off clothes as they run, especially in a race where it's cold at the start. Here though, I kept my hat and gloves on the whole time, and I had a extra few layers as well.

I've had a few problems with customs over the years, but never on the way to the states. They'd ask me what was I doing over there, I'd tell them I was doing a marathon, and sure they could see I was coming back in a couple of days. Every time you go, security gets tighter.

Tiberias Marathon, Israel, 2008

I got awful hassle at the airport in Tel Aviv. I was on my way out towards the arrivals gate and the customs guy calls me over and starts going through my stuff. He asked me what I was doing there, and I took out the racing magazine I had with me and explained that I ran marathons all over the world.

I carry this thing in my bag called a volumatic spacer. It's a big thing shaped like a bottle that I use with an inhaler. I need it for my asthma. When it comes up on the scan, it looks like a bottle, and of course you're not allowed through with bottles anymore. They were all about this and what was it and what do I use it for. I had to take it out and explain that it helped my breathing and do a little demonstration for them.

They let me off eventually, but they must have had me there for half an hour, asking all kinds of questions.

When I got to the hotel, it was crazy busy, and I couldn't check in for more than an hour. But the good thing was that the starting line was just outside the door. The race itself went grand. The course ran out alongside the Sea of Galilee. There was a very big military presence all the way along, soldiers up on the roofs and everything.

Marathon Philippines, Manila, 2008

Conditions were awful in Manila. It's a very poor city and you could see evidence of it everywhere.

This was another pre-dawn start to keep out of the sun, but it was very muggy. Humidity was high. I ran the first sixteen miles but I had to walk the last ten, on and off. I was sweating hard. The whole thing took me six hours.

Stevenage Marathon, England, 2008

Myself and Colette in the running club have a friend in England, Roger Biggs, who's also done 100 marathons. He's chairman of the 100 Marathon Club in England. Stevenage is his home club, so we said we'd go over the do the run to support him.

This was another off-road job, and they can be enjoyable, but they can be difficult too. It's grand if it's straight forward and well-marked, but I don't like it when the turn offs don't jump out at you. If you're out in the middle of nowhere and you don't know where you're going, that spoils the day. You're worried you might get lost – you probably won't because someone will call you back – but it's always on your mind so you can't enjoy it as much.

I stayed with a group of runners, on and off, and it was over turnstiles, turn left, turn right, all of that kind of thing. You had to check in at certain points to make sure you were keeping up. I was happy to go over and support Roger, but I don't think I'd do this sort of run again.

Zagreb Marathon, Croatia, 2009

Cobblestones are a curse on a marathon, and the one in Croatia was all cobblestones. They nearly killed me. My knees were very bad after it. It was an out-and-back marathon, where we ran 13 miles out of the city and then ran 13 miles back. I ended up having to walk long stretches of it because of the effin cobblestones.

Newry City Marathon, 2009

Newry was a disaster. I think I probably overdid it in 2008 and 2009. I had the end in sight and I think I pushed myself too hard. When you do that, you pick things up, and I kept getting chest infections.

Newry was another out-and-back marathon, and I was coughing and choking all the way through it. Then, at the end, it started to rain, and that didn't help either. I ended up having to walk half of it. I did a lot of walking on those last ten. I just had to finish them.

Dingle Marathon, 2009

Number 97. I was fine the week before Dingle but I must have gone out and got wet, because after five miles, I felt terrible. I was running with a friend of mine from the club who drove me down. I suffered that day, and the following day I couldn't talk, I was that hoarse.

It was a tough course too. There was the mother and father of a hill at 20 miles. It's very, very steep. There's a fella called Gerry Forde from Cork, he uses a wheelchair, and he had to get someone behind him to shove him up the hill and keep their foot on the brake. I finished it, but it wasn't easy. I met my doctor in Loughrea the following day, but I wasn't even able to talk to him. My voice was gone.

Mumbai Marathon, India, 2009

It was very warm in India, and it was one of those places where they wouldn't leave you alone. I tried to go out for a walk, but there were people coming up to me the whole time selling me this and selling me that, or trying to bring me around the place in a horse and cart.

I had big problems with the taxi. I booked one in reception to take me to the start of the race because it was a good bit out from the hotel. It never showed up. So I went to the doorman and told him the story and he rang someone else. But this guy fleeced me. At that stage it was late and I couldn't wait for anyone else, so I paid what he asked. But later on, I reported the guy to reception. They asked me if I wanted to make a formal complaint, but I had the guy booked to bring me to the airport the next day and I didn't want the hassle.

The following day, your man had a very different attitude. He asked me to write a letter to the hotel saying everything was ok and that I was happy with him. The cheek of him! 'I could get fired, I could get fired!' He was saying.

'Good enough for you,' I said to him, ' I'm not writing any letter.'

Nashville Marathon, 2009

Up there with San Diego as one of the hottest ever, around 30 degrees most of the time. I had to stop at 20 miles and walk. But I finished it.

Niagara Falls International Marathon, 2009

This was number 99 and it was a nuisance. Niagara Falls is right on the Canadian/American border, and you can approach it from either side. The race starts in Canada and you run into America. I landed in America, and on the day before the race, I took a bus over to the Canadian side to register, so I had to go through customs and all that. Then on the morning of the race, it was the same thing. We were all on the bus and the fella from customs got on and went through everyone, and of course it was the same coming back.

The race itself went badly because I got cramp and no one could help me. Normally they'd have first aid stations along the route, and there'd be someone who'd be able to spray something on your leg, or give you a massage to loosen it out. Not here though. They told me there was some fella going around on a bicycle that could help, but there was no sign of him, so that was no good to me. Their solution was to jump into the car, which was the last thing I wanted to do. When I got home, I got my sister to send them an email, telling them I wasn't happy about it.

This was all the wear and tear, all the marathons catching up on me. I ran to 13 miles, then the strategy was walk a mile, run a mile, and eventually I got there, but I was pissed off. I still finished it, but it took around six hours.

Run Barbados Marathon, 2009

I wanted the last one to be special, I wanted it to be somewhere different. But I wouldn't have gone on my own. My friends Colette and Noel have a friend in Barbados, and they go over every year to do it, so that's why I picked it to be the hundredth. Otherwise, it would have been Dublin. I asked my brothers could they make it, but it was just too expensive, and taking time off work isn't easy. They've been there for me for lots of other marathons, and I've always appreciated that.

But because Colette and Noel were there, it meant I had people to celebrate with after, and that was important. So I took some holidays and got there a few days before the race, and stayed a few days after as well. I got a place by the beach, and there was pool there too. By the time the race came round, I was well rested.

They bussed us into Bridgetown, the capital, for another early morning start, but it was still very warm. I ran a bit and walked a bit. After Niagara, the 99th, I'd taken a bit of a break and got a massage, but there was still a lot of mileage on the clock, and I was feeling all of those races.

I had a singlet specially made for the day. It said 'My 100th Marathon, Barbados' and the date. People were going 'Wow' and wishing me luck. One fella wanted his photograph taken beside me.

It was great to finish it, to get it done. I thought those chest infections earlier in the year were going to set me back. If I hadn't finished Newry or Dingle, Barbados would only have been No.98 or No.99. That would have spoiled everything, it would have meant putting off the hundredth for another year.

At the end, Colette and Noel presented me with a beautiful piece of crystal that they had inscribed with my name. I was delighted with that. I was delighted too to be able to do it in Barbados. Some people asked me, 'Why didn't you do the last one in Dublin?' But no. When people ask you where did you do the hundredth, you don't say Dublin, you say Barbados. I like that.

Made in the USA
Charleston, SC
25 February 2014